# A is for Affrilachia

Copyright © 2023 by The University Press of Kentucky

Scholarly publisher for the Commonwealth,
serving Bellarmine University, Berea College, Centre
College of Kentucky, Eastern Kentucky University,
The Filson Historical Society, Georgetown College,
Kentucky Historical Society, Kentucky State University,
Morehead State University, Murray State University,
Northern Kentucky University, Spalding University,
Transylvania University, University of Kentucky,
University of Louisville, University of Pikeville, and
Western Kentucky University.
All rights reserved.

Editorial and Sales Offices: The University Press of Kentucky
663 South Limestone Street, Lexington, Kentucky 40508-4008
www.kentuckypress.com

Cataloging-in-Publication data available from the Library of Congress.

ISBN 978-0-8131-9637-4 (hardcover)
ISBN 978-0-8131-9638-1 (pdf)
ISBN 978-0-8131-9639-8 (epub)

This book is printed on acid-free paper meeting
the requirements of the American National Standard
for Permanence in Paper for Printed Library Materials.

Manufactured in Canada

Member of the Association of University Presses

# A is for Affrilachia

Written by
Frank X Walker

Illustrated by
upfromsumdirt

UNIVERSITY PRESS OF KENTUCKY

A is for *Affrilachia*, **Alabama,** Asheville, and Alcoa, **Tennessee.** Addie Mae Collins—one of *the four* little girls killed in the bombing of the 16th Street Baptist Church. Angela Davis and August Wilson, the Hill District playwright who wrote ten plays about **African American** life.

B is for **Booker** T. Washington, *Blackberries*, *Blackberries* by Crystal Wilkinson, and the **Blue** Ridge Mountains. **Bluefield**, **Berea** College, **Birmingham**, the **Banjo**—born from Africa's akonting—and **Bessie** Smith, Empress of the **Blues**.

is for...

CARBIDE LAMP

C is for Coal Camps, Company stores, and Carbide lamps. Chattanooga and the Carpetbag Theatre. Chadwick Boseman and the Carolina Chocolate Drops. Carole Robertson and Cynthia Wesley, two more of *the four.*

D is for the real **Dukes** of Hazard and Denise McNair, the *fourth* little girl killed in the bombing of the 16th Street Baptist Church.

is

for...

Encyclopedia of Appalachia

**E** is for **E**dward J. Cabbell, coeditor of *Blacks in Appalachia,* **E**nvironmental justice, the *Encyclopedia of Appalachia,* and **E**ffie Waller Smith, an early twentieth-century poet.

# F

is for Ferrum, *Virginia*, Roberta Flack, and *Fences*.

L is for... Roberta Flack

is FOR...

GEM OF THE OCEAN

G

$\mathsf{G}$ is for **Georgia** and **G**reensboro. Funk master George Clinton, *Gem of the Ocean*, Henry Louis **G**ates Jr., and both of Romare Bearden's **G**rannies.

# H

is for the **H**awk's Nest Tunnel tragedy. The **H**ighlander Research and Education Center, **H**untsville, and **H**arpers Ferry, where John Brown made **H**istory.

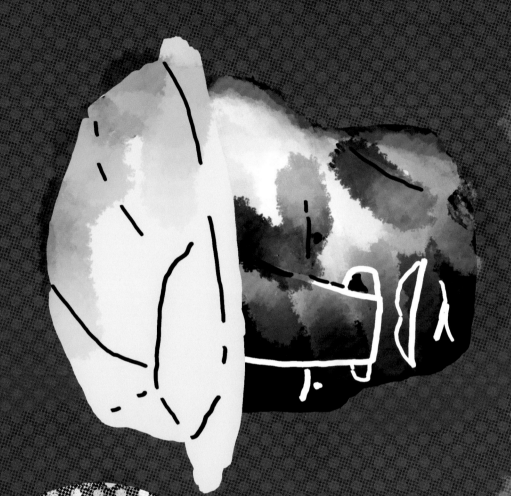

H is for...

I is for **I**-64, **I**ron ore, and the **I**ndustrial Revolution. **I**nstitute, home of **West Virginia** State University, one of the original nineteen land-grant institutions to become an HBCU, a historically Black college and university.

J is for *Joe Turner's Come and Gone*, *Jitney*, Josh Gibson, John Henry, the original steel-driving man, Johnson City, and T. D. Jakes.

K IS FOR...

GURNEY NORMAN

KINFOLKS

**K** is for *King Hedley II*, *Kinfolks*, Karida Brown's scholarship, and Amythyst Kiah's chords and keys.

# L

is for **Lynch, Kentucky,** "Lean on Me," and metal **L**unch buckets.

M is for...
Mountaintop
Removal

M is for **Mississippi** and **Maryland**. *Ma Rainey's Black Bottom*, resisting Mountaintop Removal, Randy Moss, Melungeons, and the 1920 coal Miners' strike in Matewan, **West Virginia**.

N is for **New York**, Nikki Giovanni, **Nina** Simone, **Norman** Jordan, and a new name for **Negro** Mountain, elevation 3,213 feet.

O is For...

LAMP

O is for Oil lamps, the **Ohio** River, and Jesse **O**wens, who won four gold medals in the Berlin Olympics.

P is for Pittsburgh, Pennsylvania, Picks and shovels, *The Piano Lesson*, **Pluck!** literary journal, the Affrilachian **Poets**, and Cool **Papa** Bell, one of the superstars of Negro League baseball.

Quilt

20

Q is for **Q**uarry tub and **Q**uilts, which sometimes had secret maps for Harriet Tubman's passengers.

**R** is for *Radio Golf*, Sparky **R**ucker, **R**hiannon Giddens, and following the Underground **R**ailroad all the way to John **R**ankin's house just across the **Ohio R**iver in **R**ipley.

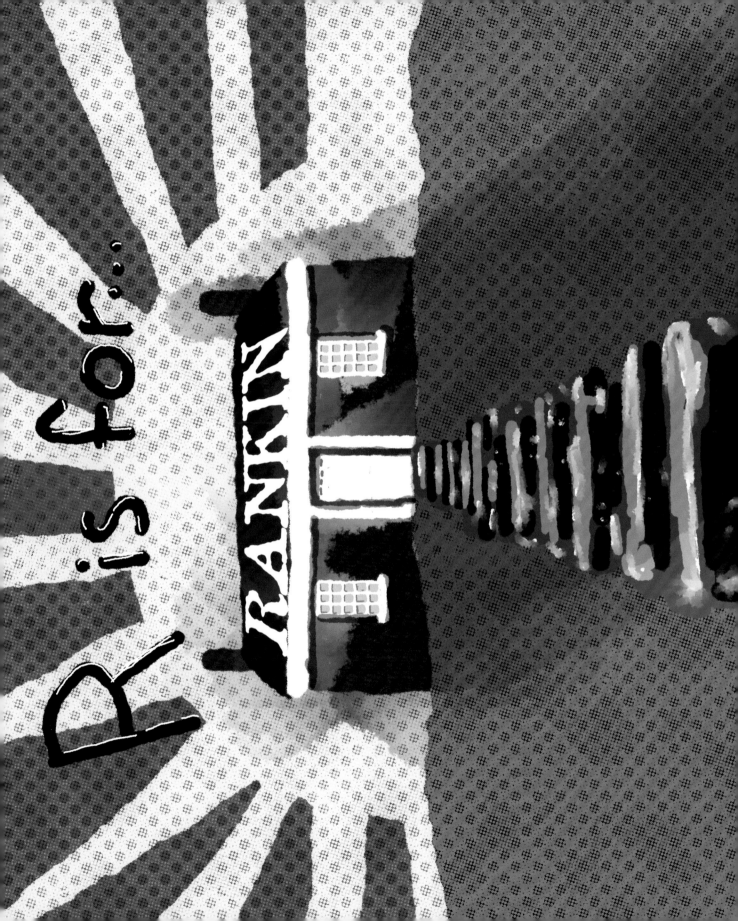

**S** is for...
**SCRIP**

TWIRLED MOUSTACHE MINING COMPANY

5¢

1619

NOT MONEY
FIVE CENTS

5¢

S is for **South Carolina**, *Seven Guitars*, **Steel mills**, and **Scrip**. Sonia Sanchez, Satchel Paige, **Sun Ra**, and **Slab Fork**, home of "Grandma's Hands."

**T**

is for *Two Trains Running,* Tryon, **North Carolina,** the *Roanoke Tribune,* Aaron Thompson, and coal Tipples.

U IS FOR...
underground

U is for **Unions**, both labor and trade.

**Underground Railroad and *Umoja*, for the Unity of**

our family, community, nation, and race.

# V

is for **V**oting rights, *Valley Girl* by Crystal Good, the **V**elvety **V**oices of Nina, Bessie, and Roberta, and the **V**erve of **V**alerie June.

**W** is for **W**heeling, Bill **W**ithers, and Carter G. **W**oodson, the father of African American history.

X

is for me and mine and how newly freed
folks signed their names.

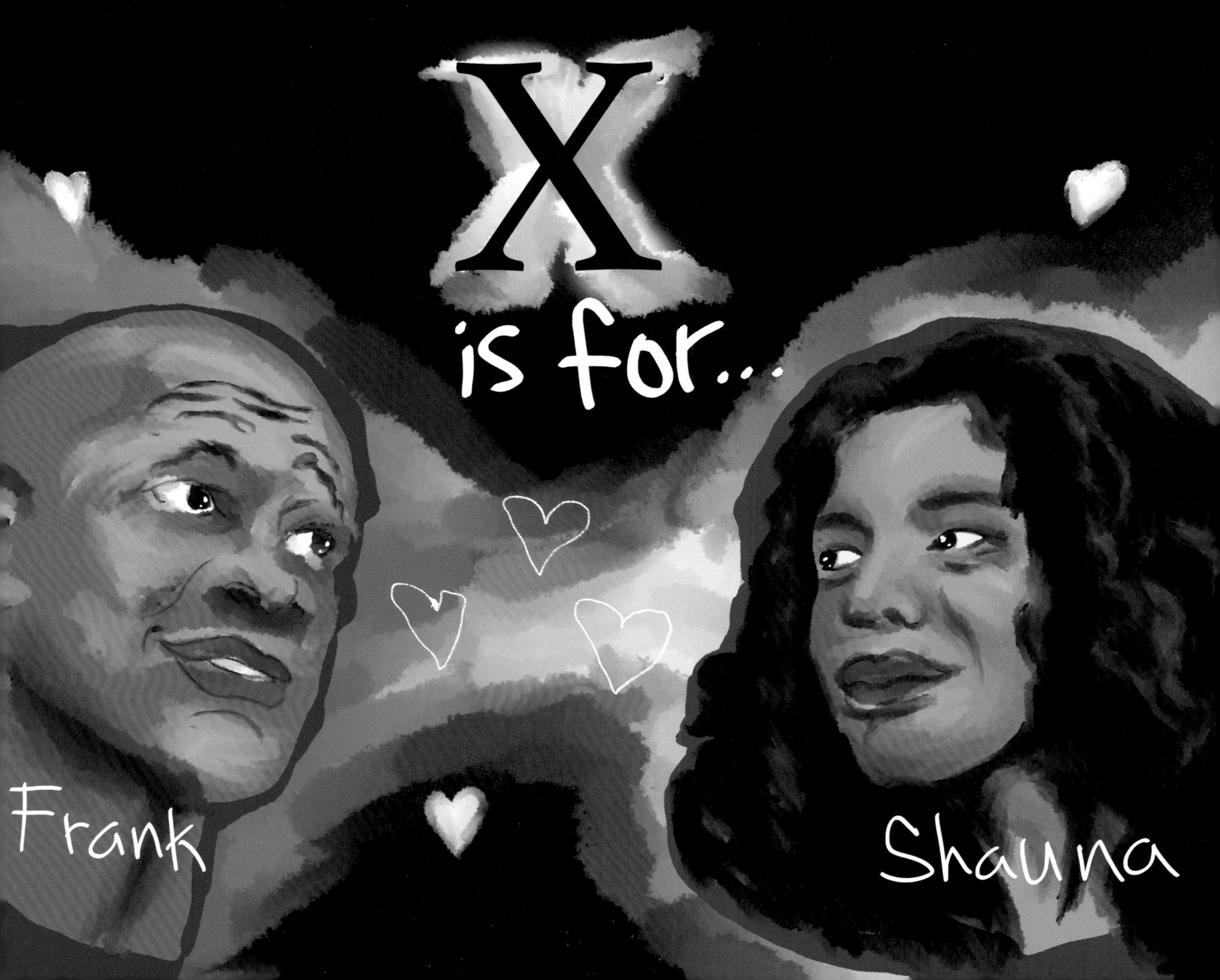
X
is for...
Frank
Shauna

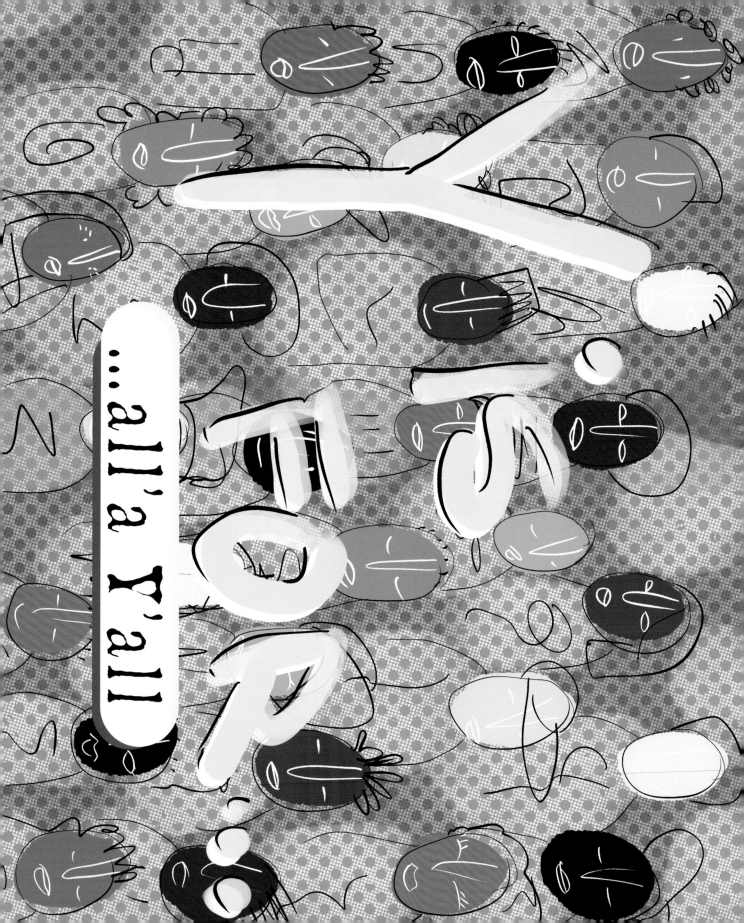

# Y is for all of Y'all.

# Z

is for cousins **Z**eke and **Z**akia, **Z**ither, the family name for mountain dulcimers, and all the **Z**zzzs you can catch dreaming about all of Affrilachia you've just seen.

GLOSSARY

*Affrilachia* is not a geographically specific space that could be identified on a map, but it is the spiritual and emotional home for everyone left out of the definition of Appalachia that requires whiteness as a prerequisite for membership.

The *Affrilachian Poets* are a grassroots group of writers of color living or working in the Appalachian region. Founded in 1991 at the University of Kentucky Martin Luther King Center, its membership includes Nikky Finney, Ricardo Nazario-Colon, Crystal Wilkinson, Frank X Walker, and others.

*Romare Bearden* (1911–1988) was a visual artist best known for collages that both celebrated and documented African American life and culture. He was born in Charlotte, North Carolina, in 1911, but grew up in New York City and Pittsburgh, Pennsylvania.

James Thomas Bell, better known as *Cool Papa Bell* (1903–1991), was a center fielder in the Negro Leagues from 1922 to 1946. He was born in Starkville, Mississippi.

*Blackberries, Blackberries* is a collection of short stories by award-winning author and educator Crystal Wilkinson. She was born in Hamilton, Ohio, in 1962 and raised in Indian Creek, Kentucky.

*Chadwick Boseman* (1976–2020), an actor and playwright best known for his role as T'Challa/Black Panther, also starred as James Brown, Jackie Robinson, and Thurgood Marshall during his career. He was born in Anderson, South Carolina.

*Karida L. Brown*, an oral historian and professor at UCLA, shines a light on black migration, politics, policy, race, and identity in Appalachian coal towns in her award-winning book *Gone Home: Race and Roots through Appalachia*. She is a third-generation descendant of migrants from the deep south who settled in Harlan County, Kentucky.

*Edward J. Cabbell* (1946–2018), a scholar, educator, singer, and civil rights activist, was the first African American to earn a master's degree in Appalachian studies. He coedited *Blacks in Appalachia*. The founder of the John Henry Memorial Foundation and festival was born in Eckman, West Virginia.

The Carolina Chocolate Drops were an old-time string band from Durham, North Carolina. Taught by fiddler Joe Thompson, their members played a variety of instruments, including banjo, fiddle, jug, harmonica, djembe, and bones, and also danced and sang. Their various configurations have included Dom Flemons, Rhiannon Giddens, Hubby Jenkins, Sule Greg Wilson, Justin Robinson, Leyla McCalla, Adam Matta, Rowan Corbett, and Malcolm Parson.

The Carpetbag Theatre is a professional multigenerational theater company dedicated to the production of new works. It was founded in Knoxville, Tennessee, in 1969 by Wilmer F. Lucas.

George Clinton is a musician, singer, songwriter, bandleader, and record producer whose musical originality helped found the funk genre. Leader of the Parliament-Funkadelic collective, he is now considered one of the progenitors of Afrofuturism. His bands and solo career are best known for their unique sound, outlandish futuristic costumes, and epic stage shows. He was born in Kannapolis, North Carolina, in 1941.

Addie Mae Collins (1949–1963) was one of four young girls killed when the Ku Klux Klan bombed the 16th Street Baptist Church in Birmingham, Alabama, in 1963.

Angela Davis is a political activist, philosopher, author, and academic born in Birmingham, Alabama, in 1944.

Fences is a 1985 play by African American playwright August Wilson. Set in the 1950s, it is the sixth play in his ten-part "Pittsburgh Cycle" and garnered Wilson a Pulitzer Prize. The film adaptation was directed by Denzel Washington and earned four Oscar nominations.

Roberta Flack is a Grammy Award–winning R&B vocalist and keyboardist. She was born in Black Mountain, North Carolina, in 1937.

Henry Louis "Skip" Gates Jr. is a literary critic, Harvard professor, historian, documentary filmmaker, and public intellectual. He was born in Keyser, West Virginia, in 1950.

*Gem of the Ocean*, set in Pittsburgh's Hill District, is the first play in August Wilson's ten-play cycle. Each of the plays chronicles a particular decade of the twentieth century.

*Josh Gibson* (1911–1947) played catcher in baseball's Negro Leagues from 1930 to 1946 and was known for his power-hitting including hitting a fair ball out of Yankee Stadium. Over his career, Gibson played for the Homestead Grays, Pittsburgh Crawfords, Ciudad Trujillo, and Rojos del Aguila de Veracruz.

*Rhiannon Giddens* is an award-winning musician, actor, and cofounder of the Carolina Chocolate Drops and the supergroup Our Native Daughters. According to her website, her lifelong mission is to lift up people whose contributions to American musical history have previously been erased, and to work toward a more accurate understanding of the country's musical origins. She was born in 1977 in Greensboro, North Carolina.

*Nikki Giovanni* is an award-winning poet and educator whose collective work is known for its calls for social justice, as well as for its tenderness. She was born in Knoxville, Tennessee, in 1943.

*Harpers Ferry*, West Virginia, became infamous in 1859 when John Brown, a white minister, attempted to use the town, the federal armory, and its munitions as a base to lead an uprising of enslaved Blacks.

*The Hawk's Nest Tunnel* near Gauley Bridge, West Virginia, is the site of one of the largest industrial disasters in American history. In the 1930s, between 476 and 2,000 men, most of them African American and denied protective gear and breathing equipment, died as a result of silica dust in their lungs.

*John Henry* is a folk hero. The original Man of Steel defeated a steam-powered rock drilling machine in a head-to-head contest only to die immediately afterward with his hammer in his hand. A bronze statue of Henry was erected outside of Talcott, West Virginia.

**Highlander Research and Education Center**, currently located in New Market, Tennessee, is a home base for grassroots organizing in Appalachia and the South. Since 1932, the center's activities have advanced the labor movements of the 1930s and 1940s, the civil rights movement of the 1950s and 1960s, and environmental, economic, and racial justice organizing across decades.

**T. D. Jakes** (Thomas Dexter Jakes Sr.) is an author, filmmaker, and the bishop of the nondenominational megachurch the Potter's House. He was born in 1957 in South Charleston, West Virginia.

*Jitney* is August Wilson's eighth play in his ten-play cycle. It is set in a run-down jitney cab station in Pittsburgh's Hill District where Black residents are forced to use unlicensed taxi cabs because regular taxi cabs will not service their community.

*Joe Turner's Come and Gone* is August Wilson's second play in his ten-play cycle. It is set in a Pittsburgh boarding house in 1911. The original title of the play was *Mill Hand's Lunch Bucket*, which is the title of a painting by Romare Bearden.

**Norman Jordan** (1938–2015) was the author of five books and was part of the Black Arts Movement. He founded the Norman Jordan African American Arts & Heritage Academy and was cofounder of the African American Heritage Family Tree Museum in his native Ansted, West Virginia.

**Valerie June** (Hockett) is a musician whose unique sound is a mixture of folk, blues, gospel, soul, country, Appalachian, and bluegrass. She was born in 1982 in Jackson, Tennessee.

**Amythyst Kiah** is a multitalented musician and singer who was part of the award-winning Our Native Daughters supergroup. She grew up in Chattanooga, Tennessee.

*King Hedley II* is the ninth play in August Wilson's ten-play cycle examining African American life in the United States during the twentieth century.

*Ma Rainey's Black Bottom* is the third play in August Wilson's ten-play cycle and one of the few set outside of Pittsburgh. Set in a recording studio on

Mountaintop Removal refers to a process of surface mining where coal is extracted from a mountain after removing the land on top of the seams. This destructive practice sends cancer-causing toxins into the air, poisons water tables, increases the risk of flooding, and destroys forests and wildlife.

The Negro Leagues were professional baseball leagues of Black and Latino players who suffered tremendously after integration. Major League Baseball now recognizes the statistics and the approximately 3,400 players who played in the Negro Leagues from 1920 to 1948.

Jesse Owens (1913–1980) was a sprinter and long jump champion who won four gold medals at the 1936 Olympics. He was born in Oakville, Alabama.

Satchel Paige (1906–1982) was a legendary pitcher in the Negro Leagues who joined the National League at the age of forty-two and helped the Cleveland Indians (now the Cleveland Guardians) win the World Series.

the South Side of Chicago in 1927, it focuses on Ma Rainey, who is considered the Mother of the Blues.

Matewan, costarring James Earl Jones, recreates 1920 union organizing that depicts coal miners' solidarity across racial lines in Matewan, West Virginia.

Denise McNair (1951–1963) was one of the four young girls killed in the 1963 terrorist attack on the 16th Street Baptist Church by the Ku Klux Klan in Birmingham, Alabama.

Melungeons are a multiracial group of people in southern Appalachia who claim European, African, and Native American ancestry. Originally thought to be Portuguese and Native American, recent DNA tests revealed no Native American ancestry but confirmed African ancestry.

Randy Moss is a broadcaster and Hall of Famer who played in the NFL for fourteen seasons with the Minnesota Vikings, Oakland Raiders, New England Patriots, Tennessee Titans, and San Francisco 49ers. He was born in Rand, West Virginia, in 1977.

*The Piano Lesson*, inspired by a Romare Bearden painting of the same name, was the fourth play in August Wilson's ten-play cycle. In the play, siblings fight over the selling of a piano that is engraved with the faces of their enslaved ancestors. If sold, the money can buy the land their ancestors worked while enslaved.

*Pluck! The Journal of Affrilachian Arts & Culture* is an academic journal that focuses on diverse regional arts and culture in the Appalachian region, including literature, images, essays, articles, and poetry. It was founded by Frank X Walker in 2007. Ed Cabbell published the first such journal, *Black Diamonds*, in 1978.

*Sun Ra* (1914–1993), aka Le Sony'r Ra (born Herman "Sonny" Blount), was an avant-garde jazz musician, poet, and leader of the Arkestra whose elaborate costumes, eclectic performances, experimental sound, and personal philosophy aligned with otherworldly ideas now considered foundational to Afrofuturism. He claimed Saturn, but was born in Birmingham, Alabama, in 1914.

*Radio Golf* is the final installment in August Wilson's ten-play cycle. It features a real estate developer seeking to become the first Black mayor of Pittsburgh, igniting a struggle between progress and his neighborhood's history.

*John Rankin* (1793–1886) was a Presbyterian minister and a devoted member of the Underground Railroad who assisted fugitives escaping enslavement.

*The Roanoke Tribune* is one of the oldest African American newspapers in the country. It was founded in Roanoke, Virginia, in 1939.

*Carole Robertson* (1949–1963) was one of the four young girls killed in the 1963 terrorist attack on the 16th Street Baptist Church by the Ku Klux Klan in Birmingham, Alabama.

*Sparky Rucker* is a folklorist, musician, historian, storyteller, and author. He tours and performs as part of Sparky and Rhonda Rucker, whose educational stories and songs consist of blues, slave songs, Appalachian music, spirituals, ballads, work songs, Civil War music, railroad songs, and their own original music. He was born in Knoxville, Tennessee, in 1946.

*Sonia Sanchez* is best known as an award-winning poet and prominent figure in the Black Arts Movement. The poet, activist, and scholar was born in Birmingham, Alabama, in 1934.

Company *Scrip* was an exploitive token system where credit was offered against the wages of workers in mining towns where the company owned and operated everything.

*Seven Guitars* is the fifth play in August Wilson's Pittsburgh cycle of plays chronicling the African American experience in the twentieth century. It tells the story of a musician who believes he is on the verge of fame and fortune.

*Nina Simone* (1933–2003), an internationally acclaimed musician and outspoken civil rights activist, was a child prodigy pianist whose professional songbook spanned multiple genres. She was born Eunice Kathleen Waymon in Tryon, North Carolina.

*Bessie Smith* (1894–1937), known as the Empress of the Blues, made a name for herself during the Jazz Age. She was born in Chattanooga, Tennessee.

*Effie Waller Smith* (1879–1960) was a remarkable Black poet who published three volumes of poetry during the early twentieth century. She was born in Chloe Creek, Kentucky.

*Aaron Thompson*, professor emeritus at Eastern Kentucky University, is the first Black and native Kentuckian to serve as president of the Council on Postsecondary Education. He is an advocate for diversity, cultural competence, first generation and first-year experience programs, and student retention. The academic was born in rural Clay County, Kentucky.

*Two Trains Running* is the seventh play in August Wilson's ten-play cycle. It is set during the 1960s civil rights movement just after the assassination of Malcolm X.

*Umoja* is the first of the Nguzo Saba, the Seven Principles of Kwanzaa. It is Swahili for unity—"to strive for and maintain unity in the family, community, nation, and race" (officialkwanzaawebsite.org).

*Valley Girl* is a chapbook by Affrilachian poet Crystal Good, whose activist work takes on controversial issues like Mountaintop Removal and the impact of chemical spills and carcinogens released into the local water table in "Chemical Valley," near her native Charleston, West Virginia.

*Booker T. Washington* (1856–1915) was born into slavery and rose to become a leading African American intellectual of the nineteenth century. He founded Tuskegee Institute in 1881. He was born in Franklin County, Virginia.

*Cynthia Wesley* (1949–1963) was one of the four young girls killed in the 1963 terrorist attack on the 16th Street Baptist Church by the Ku Klux Klan in Birmingham, Alabama.

*August Wilson* (1945–2005) was a playwright who chronicled the African American experience in the twentieth century in a cycle of ten plays. He was born in Pittsburgh, Pennsylvania.

*Bill Withers* (1938–2020) was a singer-songwriter and musician. Though Withers was only active as a musician from 1967 to 1985, his iconic songs have been covered by top musicians like Jill Scott, Willie Nelson, Kirk Franklin, and Will Smith. He was born in Slab Fork, West Virginia.

*Carter G. Woodson* (1875–1950) was considered the father of Black history. The son of formerly enslaved parents, he dedicated his life to educating others about the achievements and contributions of African Americans. He attended Berea College and the University of Chicago, and became the second African American to earn a doctorate from Harvard. He was born in New Canton, Virginia.